בס"ד

Eli Learns About New Things

Olive Oil Burning Bright is a Very Holy Light

Written by: R. Gold
Illustrations: Nechama Leibler
Translation and Rhymes by: Shoshana Lepon
Designed by: Rachel Yagelnik

goldbsd@gmail.com | goldbsd.co.il

Eli helps to clean
on Friday afternoon
and Mommy will light
the Shabbos candles soon.
Daddy fills the cups
on the candlesticks
with pure olive oil
and tiny cotton wicks.

Next Friday,
Eli wants to make a surprise.
Mommy and Daddy
won't believe their eyes!
He wants to pour the oil
so the lights will be ready
but the slippery bottle
is hard to keep steady.
Now the clean floor
has a puddle of oil.
Instead of helping out
all he did was spoil…

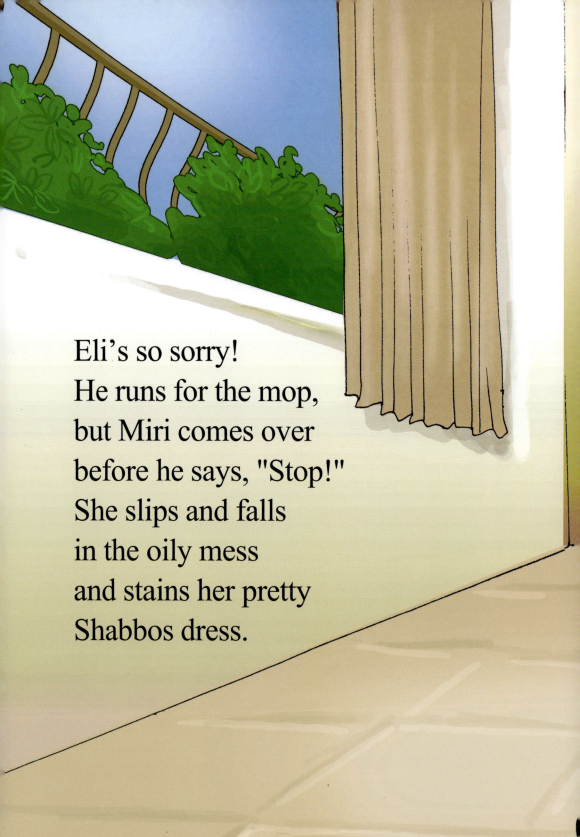

Eli's so sorry!
He runs for the mop,
but Miri comes over
before he says, "Stop!"
She slips and falls
in the oily mess
and stains her pretty
Shabbos dress.

Mom hugs Miri, and tells Eli, "I know, you really like helping, but even so, pouring the oil is a hard thing to do. Next time wait till Daddy's with you."

Miri feels sad and Eli feels bad.
What will make the children glad?
Mommy says,
"Kids, next week, let's go see
how oil is made from the olive tree."

In the grove,
the olives are ripe to pick
and they shake the branches
with a long stick.
The olives start
to tumble down,
filling up large sacks
on the ground.

Now they go to the crushing stone
where a man works so hard, all alone.
He mashes the olives
until they're ground,
and Eli helps him
go round and round.

Then to the olive press
they dash
where heavy weights
squash the bags of mash.
And what comes out
of the tiny holes?
Pure olive oil
to be bottled and sold.

The Kohen Gadol used this oil
to fill up the Menorah
and from the Beis Hamikdash
would shine the light of Torah.

Today, Shabbos candles glow so bright
and Hanukkah Menorahs fill the night
with olive oil's golden light.
Oh! What a special, holy sight!